The Hawk's Dream
and Other Poems

. . . something Chuang-tzu said, to the
effect that "When I was asleep, I
dreamed I was a butterfly. Now that I
am awake, I do not know whether I am
a man who dreamed he was a butterfly,
or a butterfly dreaming he is a man."

—CHARLES A. LINDBERGH

ALSO BY DONALD EVERETT AXINN

Sliding down the Wind

The Hawk's Dream

and Other Poems

DONALD EVERETT AXINN

THE GROVE PRESS POETRY SERIES
EDITED BY ROBERT PACK

GROVE PRESS, INC./NEW YORK

First Edition 1982
First Printing 1982
ISBN: 0-394-52828-X
Library of Congress Catalog Card Number: 82-48002

First Evergreen Edition 1982
First Printing 1982
ISBN: 0-394-62419-X
Library of Congress Catalog Card Number: 82-48002

Library of Congress Cataloging in Publication Data

Axinn, Donald E.
    The hawk's dream and other poems.

    (Grove Press poetry series)
    I. Title.
PS3551.X5T7 1982   811'.54   82-48002
ISBN 0-394-52828-X   AACR2
ISBN 0-394-62419-X (Evergreen ed.: pbk.)

Manufactured in the United States of America

GROVE PRESS, INC., 196 West Houston Street, New York, N.Y. 10014

THE GROVE PRESS POETRY SERIES
EDITED BY ROBERT PACK

To Joan

for knowing these poems
and where they came from

I am grateful to the editors of the following
publications in which some of the poems in
this book first appeared:

The New York Times
New England Review
Writers Forum
Poetry Now
Confrontation
C.W. Post College Collection
Fire Island News
Newsday
Middlebury College Magazine

With gratitude to

Grove Press, Barney and Lisa Rosset,
for this new series, and to
Robert Pack, Editor

also to The Bread Loaf Writers Conference
for the Tennessee Williams Fellowship,
which aided in the writing of
some of these poems.

CONTENTS

INTO THE WINDS

DREAMS

Prayers

I had to set limits to knowledge
in order to make place for faith.
—IMMANUEL KANT

SATURDAY NIGHT ON THE DESERT, MARCH, 1938

The moon is fully turned on over
Fort Huachuca. On a distant ridge
A coyote yaps and whines his serenade
To an audience of barrel cacti.
The scooped out valley south to Naco
Looks like the Copernicus Crater,
Scarred with faults and bouldered rubble.
Tonight Bisbee must be an erupting
Volcano of beer. The copper miners are
Rolling in the lava, its froth washing
The dank and grime from their eyes.

In this last hour before taps,
The all-black cavalry battalion
Re-polishes its boots for the Colonel's
Weekly Review on the parade grounds.
Ernesto lies against a very old fig tree,
Dreaming a cowboy's dream of Nogales' whores
With perfumed smiles and swooshing skirts.
Soon he mounts his horse, heading west
Up into Carr Canyon where that lost
Calf might be. And the coyote leaves
The ridge, following a faint scent.

CHANGES OF THE WIND

When the wind comes from the northwest
The sun-glazed grass-tops lean crosswise to
The moors and up the back of the dunes.

These tanned dancers sway, waving
To the ocean made flat in the lee.
A house fly walks on his double legs

Across the deck and yesterday did
The same thing on the other side
When the wind came from the south.

The northwest wind blows away from shore
And I can lay the seine net on the sand bar
Without the heavy surf to fight.

But yesterday's wind shifted again
Bringing the fog that hid the three
Marker-flags and made me unsure.

I call in for the weather and reports
Of a storm-line get me and my partner
Launched in our small double-ended,

Surf or no surf. First we capsize
Then force ourselves through the breakers.
Maybe there are fish waiting to play

Their part in this ancient ritual.
The sun hides behind the thick gray fog
That is like flour rolled out on the sea.

I could have taken a hint from the terns
And gulls who have disappeared. I usually
Watch these winged priests for signals.

I find the flags and anchors
And yell in triumph. There is food for the table
From the sea, gathered with my hands.

The long row against the wind seems unreal;
The sound of the surf is the only beacon
That guides me back to the firmness of land.

SOFT SUNDAY MORNING

Soft morning sags under
A ceiling of folded clouds.
The gray quiet of winter
Settles onto the slate-blue
Bay below and only the loon
                knows what to do.

A brown boulder struggles
In the waves. Hunters hunch
In their camouflaged boat,
Gulp a last drink, pull in
Decoys that must have warned
                Their look-alikes.

A pair of church-going black ducks
Amble by, casually sniffing
For something to eat.
The last of the oak leaves wiggles
For the last time and drops, doing
                graceful slips in the wind.

There should be more, music perhaps,
The sweetest strings ever played
By branches, special sounds
That hug this place of peace,
This sunday morning,
                this soft sunday morning.

INDIAN SHELL RING LOOP TRAIL

Soft Spanish moss, green and sometimes gray,
    like spider webs thrown into branches
    for drying out, are romped in
    by squirrels and formed into nests.

Oak leaves polished and glazed by the sun,
    hatch those dirigible-shaped acorns
    that boat-tailed and bronze grackles
    scatter with a racket as bad as
    arguments in a chicken-coop.

Pine cones, ready to burst and pop,
    birth wing pods by the thousands,
    ferrying seeds to the moist forest floor,
    that browned hideaway where deer
    seek roots rich with pitch, where moles
    and mice watch for fox and bobcat.

Old rice fields, now sawgrass, broomsedge
    and dogfennel, are mixed with sausage-headed
    cattails, winged sumac and black willows.
    Slaves converted these savannas with whips for
    their songs to escape the pain; then the Blues
    and Grays took turns burning the rice lands.

Boggy Gut soon rounds into view, its light shut off
    by Southern magnolias spreading low
    to keep out the sky, its water brandy-colored
    by leaves returning to the soil; and here
    on The Trail there's possum fur next to
    fox droppings that mark territories.
    A wild turkey races into the brush; an enemy is near.

Gator Point, where Old George lives,
    seems so calm now that he's taking in the sun
    that the turtles and coots go about
    their business as if he wasn't there.

Picnic Hammock, spotted with palmettoed islands,
    is a sea of salt myrtle and beaches of ferns
    that surround it like a bay spotted with
    green-sailed ships anchored off-shore.
    The old rice fields of Vanishing Swamp
    have vanished, colonized by plains grasses,
    succeeded by bayberry, green and aromatic,
    once used as an herb and spice;
    warblers, mockingbirds and cardinals,
    passing through the berries,
    drop pits that root in the spring.

Indian Shell Ring Loop Trail leads me last
    to this place where through the quiet
    of late afternoon I am back with my brothers,
    sitting cross-legged, part of the ritual:
    we are the young braves waiting for the oysters
    of the harvest. The mound of shells behind us,
    symbol of honor, makes an almost perfect circle.

"MOUNTAIN THAT WAS GOD"

"I am Gray Fox. I live and fish
the Nisquaddy and the Yakima.

My grandfather told me of Rainier,
'Mountain that was God,' land pushed
so high men would see her forever.

My grandfather told me when the rains stop and
it is clear, I will see her haloed head poking
through quilted blankets of clouds.

I will see her shoulders are the bulging
muscles of her blue-iced glaciers.
I will see her spines rise like the dinosaur's into

Rocky spires that punch through fields of
fractured snow; I have stood on her
bouldered chins, trying to understand.

Her cheeks are craggy with cracked callouses;
grandfather told me the tales of how she has been
burned by centuries of the Sun's gas-fired breath.

It is good when she is calm and pleased
with us; then there are many salmon."

SALMON RUN

years
after   swimming out of   the sweet
into   the salt
years
after   wandering   the North Atlantic
circling   fighting   surviving

    I
    flash   through rivers
    threaded   with claws
    men   then bears
    try   to   tear me
    my   pink flesh
    bleeds
    dripping   hurting

I
am   flopping   back   home
safely
to   streams
calmer
at   their beginnings

    I
    sense   you   waiting there
    in   the shallows

your eggs   all
plumped up   you
swish   your rainbowed tail
we   slip   into the pit
we   mate   I   leave

PROMISES

The others? They're busy elsewhere.
Come, rest on this blanket and
share the evening with me;
only crickets tell our time.

Whisper your wishes
and you shall hear mine,
whimsys, bubbles and vapors
kept in my eyes and ears.

If you quiver
it is from the breeze
pungent with honeysuckle.
I shall fold you into myself.

Breathe deeply, close your eyes;
I have been waiting for you!
I shall make promises
I promise never to make again.

DUCK HOLE, ADIRONDACK WILDERNESS

FOR PER MOBERG
AND DICK GREEN

I sit here on the edge of
Duck Hole, unravel my clothes
And warm my September self.

This water is bluer
Than the sky. The wind rests
And cradles the surface

That mirrors cobalt-colored
Mountains, their ridges sharply
Silhouetted against

The rich painting of blue air.
Some trees are splashed with
Reds and yellows;

Fall has started to play out
Its hands. There are no birds;
It is silent except

By the dam where the lake
Spills over and is blazed
By the sun into silver velvet.

The thin sheet curves out
Until it is pulled down
By the stream waiting below.

The wind wakes and makes
The surface shiver, blurring
The two surrounding mountains:

The few clouds that have
Come to visit are quickly
Shooed away.

A tiny island rises out of
The water, trying its first
Swim across Duck Hole.

A yell from companions
Around the point: tonight is
Sixteen miles away,

Up the Calamity Brook Trail,
Pioneered by white-rumped deer,
To a lean-to, maybe, at Colden.

The wind schemes and shifts,
Tugging fat clouds that darken.
Tomorrow we will find snow on Marcy.

Travels

A good traveler is one who does not know
where he is going to, and a perfect
traveler does not know where he came from.
—LIN YUTANG

TRAVEL IN MY BORROWED LIVES

The mist blushes,
Then curtsies to a sun
That climbs over and commands
These hills frosted with bird calls.
There is a smell this morning of
Chekhov's *The Cherry Orchard.*
        See,
There Ranevskaya and Trofimoff,
Rocking back and forth
On the plains of their lives,
Palms open,
Unwilling to listen as the old order changes
And unable to stop the sale of their heritage.

        Or, across the planet,
The set of *Gone With the Wind.*
Cocky young men gallop up to
Tara, pushing aside nests of
Magnolia mossed on their faces,
Hot to drink juleps three centuries old.
        If you prefer,
Peach blossoms dripping on Rhett Butler
Laughing on his magnificent
Black stallion; dark, grinning
Rhett Butler pouring sweet songs
Through his moustache and owled smile.

He gives a damn;
He imagines Scarlet chattering
With her suitors; but she is not
Penelope, nor is he Odysseus.

How perceptive and
Almost imperious you are to have
So much of these places in you. And
Your clothes, they're crisp and fresh like
The earth under your feet; you have
Hung up your rector's collar and dance
Pink waltzes, sweat satin gavottes,
Or jump into blackened boots, down on
Your haunches, doing the kazotsky.
Go anywhere with your passport of
Green optimism; Raleigh carrying
Scented letters from Elizabeth
              on your heart of whispers;
Your rapier need never be used.
You have your royal commission!

You love this path of swollen leaves
Fused with all your remembrances;
It leads up and down through old Stuart
And Tudor lacework villages. Cobblestones
Echo horseshoes prancing around the village
Square; well water glistens sweet and pure;
Apple pies cool on window ledges for
Lovers who will traffic with
Bodiced and bonneted maidens gossiping inside.

Keep on going,
Dreamer, around to the bells of this
Church tower, gothic and pointed
Like your purpose; engrave a prayer
Skipped out of France on your way back from
The Crusades.

I do know you!
We have spilled portions on stories we have
Digested, tales caked in the mud of travels,
Epics washed in the salt of Malta;
Our ship skated across Styx and Cocytus
On winds poured into jeweled goblets,
Winds of red wine that tasted like
Blood, but we did not know the difference.

Take off your dented
Armor, sit a while; there's a cardinal
With a message: his wife hides from us.
She was warned against the cossacks,
Against the gray-coats and blue-coats of
Gettysburg. She is Armenian and runs from
The Turks; she gathers her children and
Gambles on America. They will lose
Their hoarseness, learn how numbers will
Carry them to the moon. They will find
All the bright places in their myths and
Walk the rails laid down by the Italians and
Chinese and Irish somewhere between
Springfield and Denver.

Yes, your grandmother
Was Armenian and a believer. Now we can
Improvise angles that complement and
Buy rectangles we will build into houses.
We will plan errors because we have not
Traveled. What? All right,
                    One last story:
Your helmet and goggles intrigue me,
Even though your jodhpurs are torn;
Yes, I know what happened after
You crashed in the jungle, searching for
Beauty. Christopher Caudwell died in Spain;
You survived your unconscious but then
                    You always do.

This morning is bright and enters
Without nightmares;
Go! Be what you want. You have
What you need. Run or walk
But don't beg. Never beg for a ride.
                    Travel on your own.

FOURTH LAKE, THE ADIRONDACKS
SEPTEMBER, 1948

The morning haze squanders its hold
After a night of hugging Fourth Lake.
In Barrett's Cove, the laugh of
A red-throated loon bounces across the water.
College campers wake up in their sleeping bags;
The smell of coffee and bacon
Rouse them from their dreams of lovemaking.
At the west end of the lake, the 7:24
Pulls into Old Forge and leaves 10 minutes late.
A gray opossum snorting with her load.

Ted Anthonson telephones Fire Patrol
Headquarters, reaches up for a torn map,
Red-marked with several triangular courses.
He will fly over forests tattooed with
Lakes brilliantly blue; they look as if
They have never been seen before.
He carefully hand-pumps 32 gallons of
100 octane gas into the seaplane's left tank.
The sound of water thrums through the pontoons
Like drums a hundred years before.
He decides not to change one of the spark plugs
And takes off, the motor coughing and missing.
The campers push off in their canoes; toward
The rain that is a gray curtain hung on the lake.

BARRIER BEACH

The beach is a vigilant guardian,
Great arms spread out, protecting all behind.
November sits on the sand, taking its turn;
The people have returned to the mainland.

The ocean is chafed by the wind and
Bares an angry face of white waves.
A handful of gulls are bounced around
So much they finally jump up and leave.

A small trawler plows a section off
The sand bar, dragging for blues and weaks.
Sometimes it drops into farmer furrows, the rigging
Appears like broken crosses on a battlefield.

White-necked scoters fly low and fast, oblivious
To the wind that is ceaseless, that pushes
The water out of the sea up onto the beach.
It does until the November moon, no longer

Amused by the wind, pulls the water back
Down into the sea, back off the beach that's
Left only with marks and remnants,
Like a lover who has come and gone.

FLIGHT 217, CHICAGO TO DENVER

We gather patiently in the waiting room;
then on command, walk into Flight Two-One-Seven,
strap ourselves down and swoosh out of
O'Hare as if flung by a giant slingshot.
The past is finished and Chicago stays behind.

We ascend without even breathing hard;
the earth is sectioned into a jigsaw,
the pieces and places waiting to be played
with the way we did when we were kids.

Underneath, Missouri; the land is pressed
into brown hills, scrunched and wrinkled
like old skin; between, farmers have
stored water into circles now frozen.

Spring will turn ice back into water,
spilled to moisten the soil; the new
season will unleash waiting seeds.
Streams have been practicing all winter
and will grow into rivers; their energy

will scourge and sweeten the land.
The sun will draw the men from their
homes; they will bite the land with
their machines, spitting out chewed-up pieces.

Down there, somewhere between the
Mississippi and Missouri, dots move
along straight lines that end in colored
clusters; wheel hubs and spokes.
Their smoky breath rises almost as

high as our silver whale. Here in
this spotless sky, we split the blue
on this path of air and quickly
move across Kansas and over plains
where no one turns the ground or

strokes it into sweet smells
loosened out of the loam; the water is
about gone; the Nebraska sun bakes the land,
heating the circles; squares
are tan and brown, like a Mondrian painting.

Flaccid rivers stretch
across the flatness, across
the plains, across Nebraska into
Colorado. They came to an end,
unable to push over the Rockies,

angry-looking, that stand up to the sky.
Fed by cattle and grain from those plains,
Denver sprawls out against the mountains.
On the ground, the day slows; we travel like ants.
Jets cross high above, pulling white lines.

ALONG THE INDIAN TRAIL

Spruce and pines stand,
Quiet spectators their limbs unraveled.
And the plains are unfolded palms of hands
Lined with roads heading off to villages

Where the mail is gathered,
The VFW, Masons and Farmers Co-ops
Hold their meetings and Saturday shopping
Draws the people together for looking and talking.

Four-seasoned valley, ancient Indian trail,
Think back; what can you tell me of other feet
That traveled slowly along this river,
Toward deer or bison or fish?

Did they see the same mud flats
Plopped with snow cakes that will soon disappear
Into a spring that paints green over the brown,
And reminds birds to stake out territories?

The weather, whose power the Indian knew,
Has small effect on us and our metal horse.
We sweep onward, the wind steps aside,
Making days hours and minutes seconds.

The Indian would see the white of the rabbit's tail,
Evergreens dump fat snow in the March sun.
If he were to ask if getting there this fast
Was better, should we tell him yes or no?

HUMMINGBIRD'S DANCE

Hummingbird morning
Creeps out of the east,
Spills into my eyes;
Rich Jamaican coffee
Washes away deep
Tropical sleep.
The coffee-dream persists,
Drifts up hot from
The raucous jungle;
Turkey vultures soar,
Floating on young thermals,
Knowing the wind.
The sun will not wait,
Splashes rainbows into
Arching flowers,
Erotic as dancers.
Light skips onto the lagoon,
Rubs cool turquoise
Into the coral reef where
Fish are chasing and chased.
My hummingbird mind
Sucks nectar that
Flows into my wings.
I stand on the air,
As if floating.

FLOATING

A curious stillness
         spreads.
I flop
down on this couch
that beds my body and
cradles my head.
      (Oh, mother,
remember when I was
little, how you held me
in our bathtub, keeping
the soap out of my eyes?)

Suspended
between waking and
         sleeping,
the sounds of birds and
bell-buoy recede.
In my fog-filled
mind, I fall
         upward,
floating to a point
somewhere near
Io and Calypso.

The stars,
         billions of them,

everywhere,
are candles
in this huge church.
Some are blue,
          even a red,
but mostly white,
like sequins
on velvet black.
Down there is
          the earth,
bluish-green,
with swirling
white blotches.
          (Is that
where I live?)

I kneel,
hands covering my eyes,
whisper a prayer,
          receive a blessing,
swing around and
wave goodbye,
falling
          backwards
through this strange
black light,
plunging, tumbling
without fear,
          floating
on this dream
I have had before,
that I will have again.

RACHEL

FOR BARBARA AXINN

And finally
you arrived,
breathless,
after waiting
for months
in the wet warmth,
becoming you
inside your mother.

And then
you cried,
that first breath
pushed through
vocal chords
you learned
could be used
from then on.

We heard you,
Rachel,
mother first,
through tears
that were the first thing
she offered you,
tears she had been saving up
and didn't know
were there,

tears
that made her milk flow,
milk
that will bond you
together as in
no other way.

And then
when she held you,
you stopped crying
because you knew
she would be yours
from then on.

And I cried too,
because already
I loved you
even though
we had just met.

I didn't
know who
you would be,
Rachel;
I waited a long time
for you,
and it was dark
where I was, too.

Talk to the Living

Fools and wise men are equally harmless.
It is the half-fools and the half-wise
that are dangerous.

—GOETHE

EVEN MY MEMORY OF IT WILL CHANGE

The sun slips off the sky
But will return in the morning.
You will not:
You died
And cannot see the orange-reds
Change into yellows brushed
With a band of green.
I cannot share with you
Tonight's twilight and
Watch together how it lets in
The robin's egg-blue.
I cannot show you
How the cobalt changes into
Indigo, then creamy silvers and grays.
You will not
Put your arm around my waist
As the colors plunge into
Ebony-black pecked with pin lights.
Even my memory of all that has changed.

We do not play in the park
Anymore, "our park."
I go there holding out my hand
Waiting for your fingers,
Remembering your blue eyes
And that day when you told me

They were my mirrors as mine were yours.
And that other time when
We launched a white stick
Covered with dandelions.
We named it, didn't we?
Even my memory of it has changed.

When was it we finally blurted out
How much we wanted each other?
And about the others
We could touch no longer.
Even my memory of us will change.
Yours already has.

It was raining when we met;
You wore that floppy hat and
A camel's hair coat with a belt,
Down over there
On that little bridge over the brook.
You said sadly, "Nothing will stay the same."
I pushed and then pulled you with both hands
Trying to make you smile,
But you looked down and saw something.
I wondered why I couldn't.
Even my memory of all of that has changed.

homage to the icons

FOR FRANCES WHYATT

your soul is on fire, like mine
so you had better think twice
you had better pay some kind of homage
everyone knows you were such a good child
you had better do exactly what they say
at least pretend you agreed with them
priests are all around you
soothsayers claiming to have the answers
doctors who play god, editors and
all those other "experts" with power
mothers and fathers sometimes

of course you will hang either way
what kind of music did you say you wanted
forget it, there aren't any choices
stop crying, those lilies there are for you
yes, the white ones from bermuda and
the tiger lilies stolen from the train station
flowers make good offerings
the slugs and ticks go with the lilies
even if you try to shake them, they still won't come off
remember the icons jim jones built in guyana
his followers really believed him, didn't they?

or if you don't like his
how about the ones down in the pentagon?
they sure worked in vietnam
it wasn't jim jones' almond tasting Kool-Aid
but from the helicopters they were just as effective
nixon and his crowd knew how to make all kinds
when you have cancer
what kind of homage do you think might work?
money will not do it, love is not enough;
time is on fire, like your soul
perhaps only idiots do have anything to scream about

MUR DES PLEURS

The Wall wails,
sways in prayer,
served by
bearded Jews in black,
black Jews from Africa,
yellow Jews from Asia,
white Jews from the Americas,
Israelis in army uniforms,
all chanting
in Hebrew,
their language of law and history,
standards and statutes.

The men bend but
the Wall
stands straight,
   as it did when
   Judas Maccabaeus
   shouted to the zealots
   across the valleys
   to enter the Temple
   and pray again,

   as it did when
   Herod watched
   Pompey and Crassus
   sack and throw
   the Jews out,

as it did when
Herod, the Edomite,
decided he was
a Jew and
rebuilt the Temple.
The Wall wails
each time
scars are cut
and fired by
intruders into rubble;
red chariots drip,
metal soldiers shout,
spoiled women scream.

Jews remember,
against *le mur des pleurs,*
their Western Wall that wails,
their Western Wall that waits for
the rest of its body
to be restored.

THE FLIERS OVER WATER ISLAND

Two jump-suited fliers wore checkered
wings and flew high on the wind like
hawks playing. They looped, belly-
wopped and roller-coastered, laughing
and doing what others only think about.

They wore feathers; the air was theirs.
Their juices ran fast and today they
were boys again, twisting and turning,
again and again. Perhaps they danced
lower than they could have, unaware.

I watched, smiling whenever I see
children play. After they finished,
gliding as if bowing, I thought of applause.
When they got lower and lower I waited
for them to open the throttle,

Hear the familiar sound of that engine
and see their plane work against gravity.
But the motor did not start, and they were
down to a few hundred feet. I knew they could
not get up again, that their playing had stopped.

These pilots knew about stalls, air speed,
Altitude, and how the wind slows and softens
landings: that is the training for birds.
They must have forgotten or panicked; they could
have landed on the open beach, hard next to

the ocean, or in the moors, even nose-high
on the ocean, now flattened by the northwest wind.
But as they glided without sound along the beach
that beckoned them, they waited too long;
they came too near the crowds at Davis Park.

I watched, trying to imagine what they
must have been saying, voices raised,
desperate, out of time and ideas.
I ran hard, shouting,
"Land on the water! Keep your air speed!"

They got lower, almost to the people. Out of
instinct, they raised the nose and tried to turn.
But the plane did not forget the rules and stalled.
It dropped straight down and buried its nose
under the sand. I made believe a summer kite crashed.

I was fifty yards away and prayed there would
be no explosion and watched for them to crawl out,
just as I watched my father do when I was seven.
The plane's body bent in half as if the tail
tried to escape where the nose was taking it.

A wheel-foot sheared off looking strange
in the sand; the painted feathers on the wings were
crushed and bits of metal lay like fallen leaves.
"Stand back! Stand back!", two of us yelled
as we dragged out one of our broken birds.

I placed a finger under the other's jaw,
as if I could press life back into him.
The first still clung to his life line
as we tried to help him up so he could fly.
But no wind would lift these two dead birds.

APPOINTMENT IN SAMARA

"... and one of them, on seeing
Death, runs away to Samara.
'That's strange,' Death says
to the other, 'that's where
I have an appointment with her.'"

I

She hears the wind
Pour through the oaks,
How it organizes the branches,
Stirring the leaves that make
A confusion of small sounds
Against each other.

I must tell her
The tree tops sway in sections
Like undulating ballet dancers
Moving in waves.
She nods and muses quietly,
"Yes, of course."

I must tell her
Of the ravens
That took her eyes,
That fly soundlessly,
One by one,
To the bird feeder

Taking turns with bluejays and cardinals,
Offering colors
She has not seen
Since she was three.

II

And a storm follows;
She runs wildly
Trying to escape
Each clap of thunder,
Unsure where the lightning
Will strike;
She bangs into brush and
Trips over stones.
I call out to guide her
But she cannot always tell
Where things are
In the darkness.

III

Sometimes she feels
My mouth and face
With her fingers.
She can tell me what I see
When I have not even noticed.
She knows more quickly

When the sun flames softly
But not where it casts
Deep tones on an aging afternoon.

At night I whisper that
She loves more fully than I do,
that less is often more.
She smiles and tells me, yes,
She hears and smells and tastes better
But that she would trade it all
For twenty minutes
In front of my mirror.

TRUE LOVE

Night has shut off the light;
The crickets are my eyes.
    They tell me the tales
    They would have me know:
Of shining knights
        On horse by the road,
        Silk scarves tied
        Tight to lances;
Of fiery dragons,
        Nicely groomed,
        All green and smiling,
        Breath smoky sweet,
    Who loved the knights,
    Who killed the dragons.

If you listen carefully
The crickets always stop talking
    At the sound
    Of approaching horses.
Some say
        The crickets see
        The knights.
That may be.
    But they don't see
    The dragons anymore.

INTO THE ALPINE MEADOW

I lean hard
Against this mountain,
Pull myself up
Step by heavy step.
My sweat steams into
The chilling fog,
A cloud blanket
Wrapping itself around
Mount Rainier pressing
My body in on itself.
I climb higher and higher,
Struggle for air;
Then, suddenly,
I break through the clouds,
Shout at the sun.
The alpine meadow runs
So wild with colors
I fall to my knees:
Red Indian Paint Brush,
Blue Lupines,
Creamy Avalanche Lilies,
Queen Anne's Lace.
And the music!
It's everywhere!

"COW," WHO SAVED ME
FROM FRANKENSTEIN

I was scared, I mean really *scared.*
We had gone to Loew's Valencia,
same as every Saturday Afternoon.
My God, what a place for fantasies,
that huge black ceiling with pin
lights for stars and the buildings
of a city (we always thought N.Y.C.)
silhouetted against the night.
Every Saturday Afternoon, two features
and serials, the ones where the good guys
never lost their hats after a fight.
There he is! Get him! Hey, watch out
for yours! Okay, now let's get
Lois to a doctor. Quick! You bet
your sweet ass: every Saturday aft.
And if it wasn't the good guys after
the bad guys or the cops after the robbers,
then we might get Flash Gordon fighting
the pointy-eared, black-moustached Ming
of the planet Zoar. We really got
into it; *we* got the bad guys. Every time.

Anyway, this particular Saturday
they showed "Frankenstein," not

"The Son of . . ." or "The Return of . . ."
but the original "Frankenstein."
I was seven and "Cow," my brother Calvin,
was ten. The story? Oh, like all of them,
he gets it in the end. But if they
made *him* once they could again,
couldn't they? And I had all afternoon
to think about it: *he* would come and
get ME that night (that's when it
always happens, you know, when you're
asleep. *That's when he gets you!*).

What did I know about Frankenstein
being real or not. You weren't
supposed to admit you were scared of
anything because you wouldn't be brave
or a "man," like those heroes
in the serials, like my father, who was
afraid of nothing. (I watched him
win fights with Polish stevedores on
the docks, watched him once crash in
the plane he was piloting—and walk away
unscratched, laughing.) Even "Cow" never
admitted he was scared. The summer before,
he and my father, going down the Grand
Canyon on those damn donkeys, peering down
thousands of feet, over the edge which
you *had* to look over. And my father and
"Cow" clowning around. Clowning around!
And me hanging onto the saddle horn
(please, donkey, watch every step, please!).

Now it was dark and time to go to bed.
There was no way to avoid it. I was

in the path of the monster, all right,
and sure as hell *he* was coming to get *me*.
We had this huge room, "Cow" and me,
(I went back years later—have you ever
done that?—everything was so much smaller),
twin beds, his next to the door (it didn't
occur to me that the monster had to come down
the hall and at least "Cow" was between
him and me), mine over in the corner
nearer the windows (I just *knew* he would
come in that way). Anyway, I couldn't
stop seeing it over and over: Frankenstein
getting up from that table, smashing
everything, creaming everyone in his way,
unstoppable. *Unstoppable* and moaning
those horrible sounds humans don't make.

Scared, you bet your sweet ass. I was
terrified! Couldn't tell my parents,
they wouldn't have understood. Besides, *men*
don't say they're scared. But *he* was coming,
all right, just as soon as I fell asleep.
"Hey, 'Cow.' " "What. What do you want?
I'm trying to sleep." "Nothing, I guess,
only. . ." "What." "Nothing." "Cow" went
back to sleep. What the heck was the matter
with him? Didn't he hear that clanking
sonufabitch, his ugly moans like a foghorn
bent out of shape, sounding his "fair" warnings?
Maybe that's what the problem was, *he* was
only coming after *me*.

"Cow" . . . "Cowie." "Now what's the trouble.
What's bothering you?" "I can't sleep."

"So you can't sleep. I can. Why don't you shut up." "I can't, I've been thinking about that movie we saw, and . . ." "Look, it was just a movie. Things like that don't happen in real life." "I'm afraid. 'Cow,' I mean, would you . . . could I come in *your* bed for a little while?" His perfect chance to slam me, get back at me for doing things to get attention, almost always at his expense. Now I had admitted I was scared. (Wouldn't my cousins and the kids in school like to hear that. They'd probably tell *the girls*, too.)

"All right, you can come in, but stay over on *that* side. And no moving around." I started worrying about his telling but then remembered the monster. "Well, are you coming over or not?" "Yeah, 'Cow.' And, ah . . . You won't tell anyone, will you?" "Cow" didn't say anything for a minute, but then, "no, I won't tell Dad or anyone. Now, go to sleep, will you?"

Into the Winds

The most that any of us can seem to do
is to fashion something and drop it
into the confusion, making an offering
of it to the life force.

—ERNEST BECKER

STILLNESS IN THE REEDS

             In January, when the winds
Are balanced,
                        there is
Stillness in the reeds. The sun glazes
The willowy tufts of the reed-tops;
                        the brown stalks
             are drained of juices.

             The ground sleeps; plants and
Animals
                        rest quietly,
Except for the bluejays and black-capped
Chickadees. Chatter pierces
                        the air;
             a squirrel scurries.

             I stand still
Like the reeds,
                        listening.

LAND OF DIXIELAND

Hey, listen: you can hear them, can't you?
There, around the corner,
those seven sounds scrambling
in the dank mustiness
of Preservation Hall.

Here, get a little closer.
That horn is Percy Humphrey's
lover, and
notes stand up,
each one like choir boys
marching with shiny icons
at different heights.

The melody oozes,
fingers tap on table tops,
bodies sway, controlled by the rhythm.

Well, they've finished
Beale Street Blues;
it hangs in the smoke,
then blends into laughter and
noises from chairs scratching
against the tilted floor.
Waiters hover like birds,
asking for drink orders before the next set.

They start again,
slowly at first,
the music shimmering like that "sexy" dancer
across the street,
who rolls her shoulders and then her hips.

Sweet Emma takes another last sip,
slides to the mike:
"... *don't the moon look lonesome*
shining through the trees?
Don't a man seem lonesome
when his woman packs to leave?"

New Orleans bards and balladers,
hear the cries of The Quarter.
And years earlier,
of cotton and whips,
run and hide.
Now it's all newly painted
even though some buildings
only have fronts:
nothing is permitted to spoil
the Mardi Gras.

But *he's* there,
around the corner,
legless,
begging on his skate-board.

He's still there.
waiting.

white wind

the wind is white
making branches
tremble and sing
their last chorals

a tug-boat
fastened and freezing
sobs black smoke
finally it stops

where are the scaups
goldeneyes buffleheads
even the gulls are gone
will the green return

will the wind be silent
will i see it
will i hear it
will the wind be green

i am hungry   i am hunting

i am sleek   my shiny scales hard
my teeth   pointed horns in rows
hones icicles   short   long
i am fast   very fast   i cut through
the water   smoothly   twisting
turning   perfectly controlled
i am hungry   i am hunting

what's that up there   just beyond
the sand bar   that thins and lifts up
the ocean upon itself   mackerel
a school of mackerel   feeding and swaying
in the angled light   they don't see me.

i'll strike   from the dark side   and
smack a path through them   flipping
and grabbing   a waterspout
they will never see coming
got him   and another   another

i am strong   my body perfect
my eyes   piercing beams
pointed fins   dorsal   caudal
i am the victor   the very best   i race here
there   watching   patient
ready to move   ready to kill
i am hungry   i am hunting

WET

i am
the male animal
who smells
your wetness
we do not
need words
my whole body
smells your oil
i will make you
wetter
i will slide
myself in you

i will explore
your wetness
my sap
my gift to you
your dew
your gift to me
words slippery
right now
our wetness
our smells

altar of conjunction

I am may's maypole
spinning arms
spread to catch
the smells of spring
my juices run fast
my senses sharpened
I seek
other scents
moistened and exposed

you I shall give you
all of my self
freed and primed
from the moment
I made my first breath
I shall probe
your mysteries
I shall learn
about myself

we shall stop here
folded as one
my instinct
is erected

on our altar
of conjunction
your fingerprints
marked on me
as mine are on you

WORDS

I struggle

        to free the words
        locked in my mind,

phantoms, black

        on white. They mill
        around, rarely more than

two lined up together.
Some are upside

        down. They fade in
        and out like

stars
above moving clouds.

        Unless I catch them,
        they seem to be

making fun of me,
trading letters

        with each other.

If I do not
I have to

        start chasing them
        all over again.

Yesterday I ran along trails
of the nature preserve.
I knew the hills, when I could
catch my breath after crossing over
the crests; I knew where to run,
where the finish was.

Along the cliff a black cormorant
beats into a strong wind;
he gambles that he will find
fish to eat in the far cove.

At home, my terrier chases
a squirrel up a tree and
tries to climb after him.
They play this game every day,
each knowing what he controls.

My words and I

                are wrestlers
                with masks,
dependents who

                must live
                together,
accepting

                what each of us
                has to do.

FOR SOMETHING TO HAPPEN

There is no person here except me.
An old herring gull stands rigid,
Staring out on this flat October ocean,
His feathers smoothed by the wind.

> he waits
> for something to happen

He watches the loon dive,
Bluefish ravage and feast; beyond
A thin line of cormorants skim the waves,
Repeating the season's ritual.

> he waits
> for something to happen

The blues boil the water,
Crowding their victims toward the beach.
The gull flies to scavenge in the wreckage,
Then looks over at me watching him.

> he waits
> for something to happen

Dreams

Within each of us there is another
we do not know. He speaks to us in
dreams and tells us how differently
he sees us from how *we* see ourselves.
—C. G. Jung

THE CLIMBERS ON RAINIER

We come misted out of Shangri-la,
A caravan of monks in sinuous dots,
Snow thrashing faces almost frozen.

We jerk forward, umbilically-roped,
Unable to see, pushed and pulled like
Cells linked in an uncontrolled reaction.

Each of us moves against Our Mountain,
Strangely bonded, as if we were all summoned
To Olympus by Zeus or to Tibet by the Dalai Lama.

Silence is total except for the crunching of boots
And sucking of air; heads get too hot, legs won't
Lift; we are not sure anymore we should be here.

Higher, we climb ever higher, every step our last.
Packs get heavier every thousand feet;
We begin to think about throwing them off.

Screams must be squelched until, from
Somewhere, music is heard, a march for
Sleep-drugged monks to step even higher.

On the glacier we see nothing in the chilling mist
Except our boots following the man in front;
We may get to the top but it no longer matters.

BIRD-WATCHING

black-backed
white-breasted
double-tailed penguin,
feet shuffling to his annual
mating dance, careful not to step on
the rounded sounds of strings and reeds

      thin white baton, an elongated
      finger, slashes lines through
      invisible half-circles
      only he can see; then,
      his long stick picks out
      notes ripened like the apples of October

now his raised wings wind in full
windmill circles, capturing tones
flung from the French horns,
passed on to the violins, over to the oboes,
around to the timpani
and back to the brass

      suddenly excited dancer
      cocks his hot head toward the bassoons,
      long-stemmed wood ibis or silly-
      looking spoonbills with their
      squashed beaks, green-ninny hairdos
      and pink bottoms;

soon Russian conductor starts to resemble
a huge bird, a black-coated Russian,
sable feathers undulating like wheat swaying
on the steppes—until the cymbals crash,
wings jerking as if to lift him—
but then he is calm again, feathers folded,

      and finally bows
      happy and exhausted
      as we both smile
      filled and plump,
      reach to Heaven
      where the music must surely go

the dream

about what happened in the dream,
i will tell you now:
first i watched myself soar from
New Mexico to North Carolina
my arms were wings my fingers
feathers that pulled me through
silken air people looked up at me
flying i wore a cape and on my chest
was a big "CM" (for CHAMPION MAN)
my super vision detected an attack
by pointed-eared warriors led by
the evil Ming from the planet Zoar
i knew what to do flying loops and
rolls shooting them all down only
later did i sneeze from all my wounds

then i floated down gently onto
my trapeze of blazing gold
in the middle of the neon-lighted
senate dressed in a velvet blue
robe with green arrows on my hat
of course i made a brilliant speech
eliminating dentists and crabgrass
which no one understood so i rented
it out on furry lettuce leaves
which we all ate with a dressing of

chopped-up book covers the senators
stood and clapped then sang off-tune
with the mongolian minstrels
i had such a good time i thought
i'd tell you

WHERE THE BAD GUYS ALWAYS WAITED

My brother and I could hear Gunga Din's bugle
Sounding the alarm outside my kitchen door
Those Arizona mornings when we gulped
Our breakfast, racing each other to saddle up.

Father would hide a smile;
Mother would catch us in flight
With our forgotten books and a kiss.
We squirmed, then galloped off to Elgin.

Suguaro cacti stood like
Saluting sentinels, pointing
The way through the arroyos,
Where the bad guys waited in ambush.

We won that daily race across the desert
Because we were the good guys,
Though we knew if we were late, Missus Renfrew
Would be waiting at the door with her switch.

POEMS

FOR ROBERT PACK

He makes them
from stories
he believes
have happened.

They carry
him around
like his mother
and father,

Sometimes
he throws poems up,
sometimes
they throw him up.

Either way
they are
no longer private

and will
live after
him like
his children

His poems
and he are
metaphors
for each other.

LIKE THE LIGHT

The light
retires
slowly
from quiet purples
in every hue.

The bay
is unruffled,
the gulls fly
home
singly at separate altitudes.

I try to watch
how the light withdraws from
the reds and grays,
how the water drops
in answer to the moon.

I will tell you
about this later.
I know
how
you will look at me.

Even in describing it
to you,
my love,
it will be difficult
to talk about.

SEAPLANE

I open the door,
climb in and turn the switch,
waking my bird from her sweet sleep,
stirring her juices,
sending electrical signals
to her wings and legs and tail.

She quivers as I press the buttons.
She opens her eyes,
her mouth widens slowly.
She coughs blue-gray smoke,
then whispers to me
in that tone I know so well.

She is fully awake;
feeling and smelling each other
warms all her parts.
I touch her
here and then there;
she responds easily, almost smiling.

She is ready
and I am too.
We detach ourselves from the dock,
floating away from everyone
and head
to where we can be alone.

We sweep our eyes all around:
the path in front is clear.
We wait, checking our bodies,
our voices, our joints.
We watch the wind
that will cradle us.

We run on the water,
spraying it aside,
a duck or goose or swan
pressing down the air
faster, faster until
we reach our best stride.

Air and water balance us
for just seconds
until we lean back,
letting go,
pulling ourselves up,
dripping.

We wind around the bay,
over the hills and buildings and people,
two as one;
we dip and glide,
rise and hide
in the fluff feathers of morning haze.

We burst ahead,
exploring,
singing the same song
that grows louder and louder
until, hand on the throttle,
straining to lift

ourselves beyond what we know,
we reach our altitude,
hesitate, shudder,
then drop a wing down,
sliding down the wind,
landing clean and smooth.

AN ALMOST WINDLESS WIND

The wind is almost windless
       as in sleep that is
       not quite sleep,
       that improvises dreams
       without winds,
       dreams of fulfilled wishes.

The wind is almost windless
       as it crosses the bay,
       gathering the weight of water,
       pushing it into crests
       that plunge into valleys soon
       to flatten into watery plains.

The wind is almost windless
       when I peer down
       from my outstretched seaplane,
       see no streaks on the mountain-cupped
       lake and know I am free to land
       in any direction I choose.

The wind is almost windless
       when I read poems that cry
       in the slackened October sun
       and only a hint of air
       wanders across my face,
       across lines of love or protest.

The wind is almost windless
        when as lovers we only hear
        each other as we roll over
        and over, carried on
        the whispered thermals we have made
        into an almost windless wind.

The wind is almost windless
        when we have said
        all we can,
        when what we still feel
        cannot be put into words
        but only held with our eyes.

The wind is less than windless
        for the dead being lowered
        on their final bed of dust;
        and for us, unanchored to the ground,
        who pull away, gasping for the breeze,
        faces turned like weathercocks.

THE HAWK'S DREAM

The sun prints
contours and edges,
defining trees,
houses, cars, people;
the shadows create
memories from a life
I may have
borrowed, an accident
that now includes me.

The wind stacks
leaves in corners,
later puffs snow around
plants, like feathers
quilted for winter
sleep; shadows
disappear then appear,
soundless gusts
from an insistent sun.

                    I am
                    spawned by
                    sun and wind;
                    each night

when day sleeps,
I dream
of a white hawk
who
dreams of me.